# Transforming Pain into Possibility:

# A Practical Approach

Real Talk on Becoming a Better You

**VASHONNA ETIENNE, LCSW**
Foreword by MARY ELLEN COLANGELO, LSW

The Center for Counseling & Holistic Services

VASHONNA ETIENNE, LCSW

Transforming Pain into Possibility: A Practical Approach. Copyright © 2015 by Vashonna Etienne. All rights reserved. Printed in the United States of America. No part of this book may be used or reproduced in any manner whatsoever without written permission except in the case of brief quotations embodied in critical articles and reviews. For information, address The Center for Counseling & Holistic Services, 642 Eagle Rock Ave. Suite 6, West Orange, NJ 07052.

The Center for Counseling & Holistic Services books may be purchased for educational, business, or sales promotional use. For information, please email the Marketing Department at info@njcchs.org.

FIRST EDITION

Library of Congress Cataloging-in-Publication Data has been applied for.

ISBN: 978-0-9967115-0-0
ISBN: 978-0-9967115-1-7 (Ebook Edition)

## DEDICATION

This book is dedicated to my mother, Jocelyn Marie Butler, who lived each day of her life devoted to her children and to the children of others. Despite her life's challenges, she supported by every endeavor and always instilled the idea of possibilities.

# CONTENTS

|  | Acknowledgments | vii |
|---|---|---|
|  | Foreword | 9 |
|  | Introduction | 13 |
| 1 | Conception, Development, Birth | 17 |
| 2 | Change Comes from Within | 23 |
| 3 | Stage One: Acceptance | 27 |
| 4 | Stage Two: Awareness | 31 |
| 5 | Stage Three: Forgiveness | 39 |
| 6 | Stage Four: Clearing | 47 |
| 7 | Stage Five: Manifestation | 55 |
| 8 | Haters, Scavengers and Copycats | 65 |
| 9 | Staying the Course | 71 |
| 10 | Teamwork Makes the Dream Work | 75 |
|  | Afterword | 83 |
|  | About the Author | 91 |

# ACKNOWLEDGMENTS

To my beloved daughter, Kira LeAnne Hassett, who inspires me to be greater and to be more. You have no idea how much you have contributed to my life's purpose. Being your mother has taught me some valuable lessons that I will never forget. One of the lessons being, "Never give up when the road ahead looks challenging."

To my amazing son, Jace Vaughn Hassett, who is the apple of my eye. Your special and unique gifts have filled me with patience. In the midst of challenges, your determination, will power, and commitment to change are the greatest motivators in my life. I want to be just like you!

To my baby boy, Sage Daniel Etienne, who exhibits moral character and strength. You came at the perfect time in my life. Just when I thought I had no more love to give, you came along and stole my heart. I love you beyond words.

To Hudson, my husband, who continuously supports my every desire. Your strength and commitment is unmerited. Your tenacity and patience has taught me what it truly means to press forward.

# FOREWORD

I first "met" Vashonna Hassett Etienne in May 2012 at continuing education workshop for social workers, "Business Planning for Social Impact." This workshop was at the end of an intensive, 3-day conference and annual meeting presented by NASW-NJ. For those people who have had the experience of participating in such a conference, many attendees are "running on fumes" by the Tuesday afternoon workshop. Attendees typically are not participating as actively as they may do in a Sunday afternoon workshop. Let me tell you – Vashonna Etienne is not a "typical" anything! She was – and is – an enthusiastic, passionate social worker and human being. I was impressed by her questions and insights. We exchanged business cards, and went back to our respective lives.

A couple of weeks later, I received an e-mail from Vashonna asking if I would like to meet for lunch. It turns out that we had a mutual professional colleague who thought we had similar goals to launch successful businesses. We met, and as they say, the rest is history.

Vashonna asked if I would be her "accountability partner." I was not familiar with the term, but soon learned that an accountability partner is someone who keeps you on your path, who points out hidden obstacles to keep you from falling flat on your face, who tells you that you've been traveling around your path in circles, and who gives a nudge to keep on moving and to try explore other possible paths to your goal.

Over the course of the past two plus years, I have been in awe of Vashonna's energy and spirit. She does not only talk the talk, but walks the walk with regard to her visions and making them a reality. We have encouraged and seen each other's businesses grow in their own ways and at their own paces. Little did I know at our first meeting that I would be writing the foreword to Vashonna's book *Transforming Pain Into Possibility – A Practical Approach*.

Although *Transforming Pain Into Possibility – A Practical Approach* is geared toward women who are desirous of moving from the emotional hurt and pain that limits them from realizing their potential, the lessons included are applicable for anyone wishing to transform her or his life. Vashonna draws upon her personal experiences and growth as well as those of the scores of women with whom she assisted in their journeys over the years.

Vashonna, as noted earlier, is not a "typical" person. She was not content to be limited in the number of lives she can touch and help transform. Through her vision, research and practice, Vashonna developed "IRIS," a five-stage program to help women transform their lives from lives of emotional pain and suffering to lives of unfettered possibilities and hopes. *Transforming Pain Into Possibility – A Practical Approach* is a tool that introduces the reader to IRIS in a practical, down-to-earth manner with ample opportunities to "do the work" of transformation.

If you are like me, you may be wondering "Why is this program called IRIS?" When Vashonna first spoke to me about IRIS, I asked that very question. My first thought was that it was a reference to that part of the eye that gives it color and is the gateway for light to the retina. My next thought was that it was a reference to the beautiful perennial plant that appears in spring and flowers in early summer. What I didn't know was that Iris is also a Greek goddess, the personification of the rainbow, a messenger to the gods and the gods' link with humanity. I then realized, upon further reflection and getting a first-hand introduction to IRIS at a workshop presented by Vashonna at a subsequent NASW-NJ conference, that IRIS is "all of the above."

IRIS is about letting clarity and light into women's lives. IRIS is about hope, beauty and resiliency. IRIS is about women learning how to get in touch with their humanity, the promise of new life after a painful, emotional storm.

Going back to the day I first met Vashonna (Hassett) Etienne, it has become apparent to me that through her work with clients, the workshops she presents, and the books she writes, this is truly a woman who is not typical, and both her business and her life make a social impact.

Mary Ellen Colangelo, MSW, LSW
Colangelo Consulting, LLC

# Introduction

Welcome and thank you for taking a step in making a difference in your life or in the life of another. Great things happen when we take a step forward.

I am Vashonna Etienne, a licensed clinical social worker, marriage counselor, and the founding executive director at The Center for Counseling and Holistic Services, a 501 (c) (3), nonprofit organization providing psychotherapy, coaching, and workshops to women, men, couples, children, and families.

As an expert marriage counselor and inspirational speaker, I inspire women who have experienced challenges in their lives to change their perspectives and reclaim their futures. Through my 5-stage strategy, known as IRIS, I have made an extraordinary difference in the lives of women throughout the State of New Jersey and beyond.

I have spent over 10 years working with women who suffer from emotional pain. When I say pain, I am not speaking of the physical pain you experience from giving birth to a child or the pain you experience when you stub your toe into a chair. I am referring to the emotional pain that stems from experiences of sexual abuse, domestic violence, substance abuse, child abuse, abandonment, divorce, the death of a loved one, and depression (just to name a few).

This is the kind of pain that I like to refer to as, "The Real, Hard Pain." This is the pain that gets you stuck--the pain that brings your life down. It is the emotional pain that so many women (and men) struggle with on a daily basis.

When I first started this journey, it wasn't easy. I made mistakes, I missed clues and cues, and (most importantly) I had to learn how to move my clients forward. My clients wanted and expected changes in their lives. They were coming to me to find solutions for their problems. I had to learn how to move them out of their darkness and into the light. Also, I had to learn how to help my clients renew their hope. This was not easy--it was frustrating. At times I felt like I was failing. Helping my clients to transform their pain into possibility was a challenge because the technique was never taught in school.

When I went to graduate school I had a vision of what I wanted to do in my future. I entered graduate studies hoping to learn the craft of providing effective clinical intervention and treatment. This was far from the reality. Graduate school taught me the foundation of the field--the foundation of social work. The professors taught me everything I needed to know, via course work, to successfully get me through school, but they really didn't teach me how to work with people, or how to conduct clinical sessions. In hindsight, graduate studies really didn't set me up for what to expect from people who are suffering from the pain that I am referring to. It wasn't easy for me. No one ever gave me the secret, or the strategy, for transforming pain into possibility. I HAD NO CLUE!

I had no clue how to be effective. I knew I was good at what I was doing and I knew I was making a difference in some lives but really, when I thought about it, this wasn't good enough for me. I knew making a difference wasn't good enough. I wanted to make an IMPACT. I wanted to be remembered for transforming lives. I knew if I was going to do this, I knew if I was going to make this happen, I would have to be different. I would have to be radical. I would have to do what so many other therapists were not doing!

Over time and after much trial and error, I noticed a pattern of transformation that would occur in the stages of each woman I had counseled. I started to notice how the change started to happen in these women and I noted the process daily after each session. It became critical for me to properly note the changes and identify any patterns of change that existed. The success of each woman was dependent on my ability to get her to open up and face her darkest fears and deepest secrets.

*"The success of each woman I counseled really depended on these stages."*

Once I identified these stages, I began to consistently and routinely implement the stages into my practice. Once I started to recognize what was really happening, I started to test it and incorporate it into each person I was counseling. I have witnessed transformation with not only my clients but with clients of each therapist on my team. When I started to notice the transformation that was occurring, I started to notice something miraculous happen.

I have seen women successfully leave abusive relationships. I have seen women be reunited with their children: children that they lost to the system, children that they gave birth to that were taken out of their arms by child protective services. I have witnessed women overcome depression and reclaim their lives, and I have even observed a shift in their thinking. They went from thinking and speaking negatively to becoming optimistic. They started to think in a new, healthy way. They started to have a new way of seeing what was once considered a horrible life suddenly begin to transform into their testimony of hope. I have seen transformation at all levels and with multiple populations of people.

The transformations that I have witnessed have helped me to stay focused on the bigger picture. The transformations have helped me to remember why I chose to live my life helping others live theirs!

*Chapter One*

## Conception, Development, Birth

The name Iris was not chosen by accident. When I was first challenged with deciding what name would best suit my 5-stage strategy for working with women, I created a list of names until I could not think of anything else. The list included names such as, but not limited to, Courageous Women, Determined, Lipstix, P.O.S.H., Patches, Lovelocks, and Kinks. I presented this list to Toufic Hakim, an organizational consultant from I & I Group who was assisting me with program development. I thought I had it all figured out and he was going to help me select a name which women across the nation would identify with. To my surprise, Toufic told me to go back to the drawing board and choose a name that is personal and has meaning.

Frustrated, I went back home, pulled out my laptop, and began typing, name after name, without thinking: Maya, Ella, Amelia, Bella, Khloe, Grace, Havannah, Isis, and Iris (amongst others). Nothing stood out to me. Nothing made me say, "Now, that's an awesome name!" The next week I went back to Toufic and presented him with my revised list. Toufic paused, looked at it, and started asking me questions about the names I listed. "Why did you choose Ella?" "What does Khloe mean?" "Out of all the names, which one do you like?"

I didn't know the answer to his questions so I glanced back at my list, and responded, "Isis. I like Isis." Toufic responded, "It doesn't sound like a programmatic name. People may associate it as something negative." Not liking his feedback, I explained that Isis is the name of a goddess, and I thought that women would identify with the name as something empowering. Toufic looked at me without expression for what seemed forever. When he finally spoke, I had a new perspective.

Toufic liked the name Iris because it stood out above the rest. He then gave me a new assignment to help broaden my perspective. This time, I had to research the meaning of Iris and apply it to my program. I recall thinking, "This man is brilliant." Toufic stopped at nothing until I broke free of my own restraints and limiting beliefs.

I had to handle the idea of naming my 5-stage strategy similar to naming a child. The concept was conceived, nurtured, developed, and birthed. Naming it was the last step in the process, and I took this step seriously. I believe names should have meaning, and I have always been intentional about how I named my children. This was no different.

After researching the meaning of Iris, I discovered the beauties associated with the name. It was a perfect fit. I immediately embraced the meaning and was eager to share it with the world. For starters, IRIS is known to have three different connotations: the eye, a flower, and a Greek goddess.

## *The Eye*

The iris is the part of the eye that gives the eye its color. Most people's irises are shades of brown, hazel, green, gray, or blue. There is a famous quote which states, "The eyes are the window to your soul." Basically, this means that if a person looks into another person's eyes, one can see the other person's hidden emotions, attitudes, and thoughts--the essence of her being. In the American culture, people are expected to look each other in the eyes when speaking. Not only is this interpreted as a sign of respect, but looking others in the eye is associated with telling the truth. A person whose eyes wander when speaking is often considered dishonest, or a liar.

The eyes have a language of their own. They are more than just a way to view the world. They tell a story of happiness, pain, love, fear, and almost any other emotion. The Iris program gives a participant a language in which to view her world, and the emotions she experiences.

## The Flower

When I did my research concerning the flower Iris, what I learned spoke directly to my program name. It is said that an Iris signifies faith, hope, wisdom, courage, and admiration. Similar to women, Irises exist in over 200 varieties and a wide spectrum of colors. This is significant to the Iris program because no two women are the same. Women vary in color, height, weight, and life experiences. Just like the flower, women are seen as a symbol of beauty, each bearing their own significance and meaning.

An Iris is more than a symbol of beauty, it is a persistent perennial flower. Irises have been found growing in some of the most unfavorable conditions. In a field filled with weeds, overgrown grass, and other plants, an Iris can be found in full bloom.

When I think of the women who participate in the Iris program, I can identify characteristics in them similar to those of the flower Iris. Some of these women live in conditions that are not favorable, that are designed by nature to choke the life out of them. These women have persevered and overcome some of life's greatest challenges. With experiences ranging from childhood sexual abuse to adult trauma, the women who benefit from the Iris program are women who rise above the conditions they are in, and strive to be more.

## The Goddess

The ancient Greek goddess Iris is the personification of the rainbow, as well as the messenger of the gods. Her role, although minor, was of importance, as she links the gods to humanity.

Iris is depicted by a woman travelling by way of a rainbow, from the heavens to the earth, delivering messages among the gods, and to the humans from the gods. Iris swiftly delivered messages without hesitation and with ease. One can surmise that she was effective in her role, as there does not appear to be any negative mentions in Greek mythology. When I think about that, I feel positive about a program that can duplicate the very essence of Iris, the Greek goddess. Just as the Greek goddess was effective in performing her duties, the program Iris is effective in transforming its participants.

The Iris program brings a message to each woman who participates. The message is one of hope, faith, and empowerment. Iris helps women to realize that despite their circumstances, and life's unfavorable experiences, they can still accomplish successes. The message is clear--Iris is that of Acceptance, Awareness, Forgiveness, Clearing, and Manifestation. Like the goddess, Iris is a symbol of peace at the end of the rainbow.

*Chapter Two*

# Change Comes from Within

Going through this transformation process has to be for you, and about you. This is not the time to start thinking about what others will think or say about the changes they will inevitably see in your life. Others will not understand your change. They will not be able to understand why you no longer have a negative mindset or outlook. They will not understand why you no longer associate with individuals who drain you of your energy, or with those who do not treat you with respect. Without hesitation, you will begin to recognize individuals who are constantly taking from you as well as those who continuously violate your boundaries.

Transformation is an individual process. When you begin to transform your thinking, everything in your life will begin to shift. You will start to see things from a different perspective. You will be slow to anger and quick to forgive because you will know and understand the laws of attraction, and the secret to living a happy, fulfilled life.

The things you want in life are all available to you. The problem is, you don't realize that your disbelief and negative mindset actually repel all that you want from you.

A negative mindset will, undoubtedly, work against your goals, and trick you into believing everyone else is the problem. Instead of transforming your own thinking and behavior, you want and expect other people to change. This belief system works to keep you in misery. There is one thing I know for certain, you do not hold the power to change people--you can only change yourself.

There is a popular quote by Leo Tolstoy which says, "Everyone thinks of changing the world, but no one thinks of changing himself." Individual transformation is extremely powerful and contagious. The beauty of it is you don't have to worry about changing the behavior and thinking of others. When you work on yourself, others will be curious, and they will eventually seek answers and guidance from you. Change is never comfortable or easy, per se. What makes change difficult is the battle within your mind. It is your own thoughts that destroy relationships, friendships, and companionships. Your thoughts dictate how you behave as well as the words you speak. You have to learn to be patient with yourself as you go through this transformation process.

The secret to living a happy, fulfilled life lies in your thinking. If you change the way you think, you will change your life. It is time to let go of the anger and resentment. It is time to take control over your thoughts. It is time to take the negative thinking off repeat. It is time to stop re-playing destructive thoughts in your head over and over again. It is time to take an active role in your transformation process. Everyday make a commitment to only allow positive thoughts to linger in your mind. Commit to expunge all negative thoughts by replacing them with thinking that reflects gratitude and love. I am in no way implying this is an easy process, and I am not guaranteeing an automatic shift in your life. If you want a total transformation, you have to be willing to consistently do the work!

*Chapter Three*

# Stage One: ACCEPTANCE

If you want transformation to occur, acceptance has to be present. Acceptance means accepting where you have allowed emotional pain and trauma to overpower your life. Acceptance simply means admitting that you are in emotional pain, that you are not feeling your best, and that everything is NOT okay. This stage is important because if you don't accept the fact that you are in pain, then you will remain in denial. If you are in denial, nothing will be accomplished. You will never get out of that dark hole, and the gray cloud that follows you around, each day, will remain there.

**"When we are in denial, we train our bodies to numb the disorder."**

Acceptance is not denial. Acceptance is recognizing the hurt that you are experiencing. It is also recognizing the pain you are experiencing from the hurt. Denial allows you to brush it off, sweep it under the rug, and ignore the signs that tell you something is wrong. When we are in denial, we train our bodies to numb the disorder. We allow our bodies to be overpowered by depression, suicidal thoughts, anger, anxiety, and fear. We make it normal to live with these symptoms, and we perpetuate the cycle of pain.

I had a client who refused to accept the fact that she was in emotional pain. She would not admit that she was suffering from the past acts of sexual abuse, both as a child and as an adult. Make no mistake, sexual abuse can, and does, occur in all stages of life. It can leave a woman feeling disempowered, violated, and damaged. My client refused to deal with the emotional scaring of the abuse. She brushed it off by saying it was done and over with, and that she could never take back what has happened to her. She made it clear that she didn't want to speak about it because the recalling of events, feelings, and negative emotions caused her to relive the acts of the abuse. I remember a time when she said to me, "What's the sense of bringing this back up? I'd rather not talk about it. I'd rather not go there because when I do, I am sure to go back into depression, and that's a lonely place to be. I don't want to be there, but for some reason, you insist on talking about my past."

*"If we are in denial, we cannot get anything accomplished."*

The truth is, she was speaking to me from a state of depression. The problem she was having was that she did not want to accept the fact that the actual pain she was experiencing was depression. She tricked herself into

## TTRANSFORMING PAIN INTO POSSIBILITY: A PRACTICAL APPROACH

believing that if she did not talk about her past, she would not fall into depression. She "brushed it under the rug." She did not want to accept that her continuous cycle of pain, and life choices, were rooted in her past. Her unhealthy relationships, her inability to effectively parent, and the absence of self-love were all tied into her depressed state. The story of my client is a prime example of what I mean when I say the failure to accept the fact that emotional pain is present in your life is a state of denial. Living in denial keeps us from accomplishing our goals of living happy, fulfilled lives.

### It's Time to Do the Work!

With that said, I want you to do me a favor. Stop reading, pause, and take a break, for just a moment. Go get a pen and paper. When you come back, I want you to write this down:

*If acceptance is not present, transformation cannot occur.*

I want you to realize that living a life of denial will keep you stuck, with no movement. You will be stuck in the cycle of pain, re-living the past over and over again. After you write it down, here's what I want you to do. I want you to look yourself in the mirror. Yes, I said the mirror, and for those of you who don't like looking at yourself in the mirror, suck it up, "put an *H* on your chest, and handle it." Be brave.

Look at yourself in the mirror and notice every detail. I want you to yell out loud the pain you are experiencing. If it is DEPRESSION, I want you to look in the mirror and say, "I commit to conquering depression and transforming my life."

If it is ANGER, I want you to say, "I commit to conquering anger and transforming my life." I want you to say it with conviction, passion, and volume. This should not sound like you are whispering or afraid. It should not sound like you are uncertain of what you are saying. When you speak these words out loud, I want you to say it like you mean it.

Whatever the pain you are experiencing, I want you to accept it, admit it, and commit to transforming your life.

Even if you are not the one experiencing any emotional pain, this exercise would be helpful to those who you know need it most. Maybe you are a clinician, counselor, or life coach who works with women who are suffering from emotional pain. I want you to have them do this same exercise. Have them look themselves in the mirror and commit to conquering anger, commit to conquering depression, commit to making a difference in their lives. Remember, if acceptance is not present, transformation cannot occur.

*Chapter Four*

# Stage Two: AWARENESS

There is a quote by Publilius Syrus which states, "The pain of the mind is worse than the pain of the body." Let us examine what he is saying. He started off with, "The pain in the mind." For the purpose of this book, that translates into depression, anxiety, fear, stress, anger, sadness, rage, and any other feeling that you can think of that does not make you feel good. He compared this mental pain to physical pain by saying it is worse to be in mental pain than physical pain. In simple terms, it is worse to be in depression than to fall and scrape your knee, and bruise your hands. What causes mental pain? Why is this so important?

*"The pain of the mind is worse than the pain of the body."*

It is important to understand that mental pain occurs when you replay, in your mind, and re-live painful traumatic events that occurred in the past. In order to move a step closer toward transforming pain into possibility, you have to first be aware of where the pain is coming from. This will require you to recall and re-live your feelings of hurt. For example, if you were molested as a child, and tried your best to repress your thoughts, it is important to know, and understand, repression is only temporary. There will always be something to resurface those thoughts. When this occurs, you are more than likely to experience emotional pain. This is the time when you want to first accept the fact that you are in emotional pain, and then understand where it is coming from.

Awareness is the opposite of being oblivious. When you are oblivious to your pain, it simply means you have no knowledge that the pain exits. It can also mean you are not aware of your feelings, or your emotions. Where there is a lack of awareness of one's emotions or feelings, there is bound to be a cycle of pain. You will experience the emotional pain over, and over, and over again simply because you lack awareness. Just because you don't feel the pain, or you lack awareness of its' existence, doesn't mean it is not being manifested in other ways, such as failed relationships, strained friendships, loneliness, or irritability (just to name a few).

> *"Being aware of where your pain is coming from is an important stage in the transformation process"*

Now that I am out of my cycle of emotional pain, I am better equipped to talk about my past. When I was 18 years old, I met my first husband. At 22 years old, we married, we had children, we bought a house together, and we lived life. Throughout our 7-year marriage, I found that I was often cold, emotionally detached, critical, and to be honest, I lacked affection, at times. Of course, there were times when I was loving, and caring, and I appeared happy, but this hardly occurred in public, and it wasn't always consistent. With this kind of behavior, I had to get to a place where I could take full responsibility for what I did.

As a married couple, we went through trials and tribulations. We went through our ups and downs and, to be quite honest, we hurt each other. After riding this roller coaster of marriage, we finally decided to get a divorce. It was hard, especially after having two kids. It was hard to conclude our 11-year relationship. After I emotionally bounced back, and I started finding order to my life, and to my children's lives, I started to tell myself some things about me that were not necessarily true.

I know many of you can probably relate to this, but you may not be aware of how it applies to you. Here is an example of some of the things I started to tell myself that weren't true. I told myself that my marriage failed because I was not emotional, I was not affectionate, and I wasn't really a "lovey- dovey" type of person. I told myself this so much, I believed it! I really believed these nasty, horrible things about myself.

I remember speaking to my cousin, who is also my best friend, and like a sister--I can tell her absolutely everything. I remember sitting on my bed, talking on my phone, and telling her that I am not an emotional, affectionate person. These false accusations rolled off my tongue easily. If a camera crew were present for this conversation, you would have bought into my madness. I remember telling her that I do not want to be in a relationship with someone who requires affection. Do you believe that? After all, humans are designed to be connected. From the moment we enter the world from our mother's womb, we seek to be held, soothe, and secure. The fact that I denied the need for security, connection, and affection, lets me know I was speaking from a position of pain.

I say this with all honesty, and remember it as if it happened yesterday. My cousin did something amazing for me that day (besides the fact of saying, "Hey, Vashonna, that's kind of crazy. Everyone wants affection.") Through her poised, calm demeanor, she reminded me of who I am, and who she remembers me to be. What she said made a lot of sense. It made the hairs on the back of my neck stand up. I literally felt a radiating, tingling feeling that sent a sensation up my spine, causing the hair on my neck to rise up.

And what my cousin said to me, I would NEVER forget. She said, "I don't think you are not affectionate. In fact, I think it is quite the opposite." She always had a way of putting things into words and perspective. Her imparted wisdom always made me listen--it made me perk up. I wanted to hear more of where she was going to take this since I have always thought of her to be such a deep, analytical person. It was in this moment, I became extremely interested. I was totally ready to learn. I was interested in knowing more about myself. What was she noticing that I had been missing?

My cousin helped me to recall my relationship with my high school sweetheart, how I loved him unconditionally, and how everyone in our circle of friends knew we were an item because I never hesitated to show him love and affection. While listening to her speak, I began to think, "Why wasn't I able to do this in my previous marriage?" I started to think about the fact that I withheld affection in my marriage, that I shut down, and exhibited signs of anger and frustration, and that at times, I was critical, and my choice words were far from uplifting or edifying.

> **"It was at that moment I realized I was oblivious to my own emotions."**

My cousin helped me to look at myself, and my behavior, in the mirror, but that was not the only thing she did for me that day. She helped me to realize that I was not an affectionate person with my ex-husband because I did not feel the same chemistry, or connection, and the same passion that I felt with my high school sweetheart. My high school sweetheart and I shared the same meanings and life experiences. We had an intimate friendship that was built on trust, loyalty, transparency, vulnerability, and authenticity. We had the same friends, grew up in the same neighborhood, and listened to the same music. Our connection brought out the best in me.

It was at that moment I realized I was oblivious to my own emotions. But the good news is, I am not alone. I am not the only one out there who has gone through something like this. I am not the only one out there who has believed untrue things about herself.

It's simple. We tell ourselves lies, and untrue statements, in order to justify our behavior. I had been telling myself I was not an affectionate person in order to find a reason for my divorce. Instead of saying that I did not feel passionate about my husband anymore, and that I did not want to be married to him, I tricked myself into believing that I was not affectionate, and that I was a cold, emotionally detached person who was unable to love without conditions.

*"Once I transformed that pain into possibility, I saw my greatness."*

LIES, LIES, and more LIES! I AM NOTHING like that. Once I transformed my pain into possibility, I saw my greatness. I saw my love. I saw my passion. I've seen the affection that I have. I am a beautiful person. I just didn't believe it at that time. What my conversation with my cousin did for me was help me to gain awareness into my OWN behavior. It helped me to be aware of why I was experiencing relationship problems, and it also helped me in seeking change for my life. It gave me hope of a new relationship. It gave me hope of a new love. It gave me hope of a new marriage. I have since realized that hope, and I am happily remarried today.

### It's Time to Do the Work!

Now that you have accepted the fact that you are experiencing emotional pain, and you have made a commitment to conquering your pain, and transforming your life, I want you to start the process of being aware. Think about the pain that you are in, and get really honest with yourself. Start to think about where the pain is stemming from. When did it all start? Did it start as a child? Or maybe after a bad breakup? Let's take a moment and reflect. Take this moment before you go on to the next stage, and think about the starting point of your pain. Where did the pain start for you?

*Chapter Five*

# Stage Three: FORGIVENESS

*"When we forgive ourselves, or the ones that hurt us, our lives becomes renewed."*

Forgiveness is a pivotal moment in the transformation process. Forgiveness is making a decision to stop letting our past define who we are. It is the next stage following awareness, and the most powerful of the five stages. When we forgive ourselves, or the ones that hurt us, our lives becomes renewed. We begin to feel the mental burden of pain get released from us, as though someone has lifted a car off our chest. Can you imagine that? Can you imagine a car sitting on your chest, and then, all of a sudden, someone lifts the car off your chest? Imagine how that feels. I imagine it feels like a big "release." You can breathe. You are not suffocating. That's what forgiveness does for you. Forgiveness helps us to focus our energy on the things that matter to us most like love, hope, peace, happiness, and our goals. Forgiveness allows us to see the world from a different perspective, a more positive perspective and not from the perspective of pain.

Imagine waking up without tension. Imagine waking up, and there's no grief, anger, or despair in your life. Imagine getting out of bed with a smile on your face, feeling energized, and completely focused on reaching your goals.

For some, this is hard to believe or imagine, BUT I am here to tell you that some people DO wake up like this every day. Some people are always smiling, happy, and living the life they want. But what about those people who are not? What about those people for whom waking up requires them to think about everything they have gone through? Some people may always be happy or joyful, but for the ones who are struggling with forgiveness, waking up can be a painful process.

Imagine being able to sit in the same room with the person who sexually abused you, and not feel sick to your stomach or full of rage. Imagine that. Imagine no longer spending your days and nights dreaming of your mother who abandoned you, the mother who gave birth to you, raised you, and then left you with someone else, the mother who left you to fend for yourself. Imagine being at peace within your home, or with your children, or with a previous abusive spouse. This is what it feels like when you truly forgive. When you truly forgive, nothing - and I mean absolutely nothing - gets in the way of your happiness.

The opposite of forgiveness is bitterness, and bitterness includes resentment. I know many people who have never forgiven those who have hurt them. Some of these people move through life with such resentment, and hate, in their hearts. They walk around as bitter sisters and brothers.

Bitterness includes, but is not limited to, resentment, hatred, violence, anger, retaliation, and everything negative that you can think of.

> ***"Chaos is everywhere and all around you because you are simply the unhappy one."***

When you fail to forgive the one who hurt you, or when you fail to forgive yourself of your own wrong doing, you run the change of going through life in chaos. You are likely to have chaotic relationships and friendships, and that kind of energy can also stir up chaos in your workplace. The aura and energy of chaos is everywhere around you simply because you are the unhappy one.

Unforgiving people spend their days plagued by negative thoughts, and engaged in negative behaviors. There is nothing positive about those who have un-forgiveness in their hearts. They seek revenge on everyone who has hurt them, and anyone they perceived to have hurt them emotionally. This kind of behavior and thought process eventually turns into disease within our bodies, and I literally mean that. It shows up as excessive weight gain, constant headaches, complicated health, and mental health disorders, particularly depression. It shows up as high blood pressure. It shows up as migraines. It shows up as eroding stomach muscles. It basically shows up as disease within our bodies. Believing that forgiveness lets the offender off the hook couldn't be further from the truth. Forgiveness is all about your healing—your happiness.

This brings me back to memories of a close friend I once had. She and I did everything together including weekend trips, holidays, and special occasions with mutual friends and family. She was like my sister. In fact, we resembled each other so much, people in our community thought we <u>were</u> sisters. It wasn't until I started experiencing betrayal, by her, that I disassociated myself from her.

There were three incidents that occurred in our friendship prior to me ending our relationship. The first incident placed me in shock. It was like a killer popping out of my closet without warning. It felt like someone took her fist and punched me right in the stomach, knocking the wind out of me. I never imagined this could have happened, and when it did happen, I did not want to believe the truthfulness of the story. After all, she and I were always together, and at no time did I think she would hurt me.

> *"Believing that forgiveness lets the offender off the hook couldn't be further from the truth."*

Months after the first incident, after I thought I forgave her, after I thought we moved on, there was a second incident. And just when I thought the worst was over, she surprised me with the third incident. My friends asked me, "Why are you still friends with her?" My family said, "Something is weird about that friendship, you need to move on." But it had to take, not one incident, not two incidents, but three incidents for me to wake up, and for me to get the picture. These three incidents caused me to question our friendship. It made me angry and full of rage. I became sarcastic, vengeful, and bitter.

# TTRANSFORMING PAIN INTO POSSIBILITY: A PRACTICAL APPROACH

I walked through life with this bitter, un-forgiving attitude. I knew something was terribly, mentally wrong, (hint: ACCEPTANCE) but I could not figure out why I was so angry (hint: AWARENESS). Although I ended the friendship and distanced myself from her, I became obsessed with wanting to know what was going on in her life so I could keep tabs on her struggle and her disappointments.

I watched from behind the scenes, but not with the intention of wishing her luck, or to pray for her, and definitely not to say to her that she was doing a job well done. It was so I could keep tabs on her struggles. I wanted to see her fail. I wanted to see her go through the pain that I went through. I wanted her to feel the pain I felt. I wanted her to never find love. I wanted her to be emotionally suffering over everything in her life.

## *"Hurt people hurt people."*

This may seem over the top, but if you think about it, it's exactly what hurt people do. Hurt people hurt people. When you have been hurt by somebody, you can literally spend all day thinking of all the bad things that could possibly go wrong in her life. That was me! All of this drained my energy, and it started to affect others around me. I suddenly didn't trust anyone. I didn't trust my boyfriend (now my husband), at the time, I didn't trust any single females, and I definitely didn't trust any female who shared the same astrological sign with my ex-friend. It got deep!

Then it hit me. I saw how I was being a hypocrite. How could I teach others to forgive, and take radical steps toward transformation? How could I prepare others to take their pain, and transform it into possibility? How could I teach people this? How could I go to my office, day in and day out, and have 45-minute psychotherapy sessions with people teaching them how to get over the pain in their lives, while I was living in pain? I literally spent countless hours coaching women to confront their pain, and I wasn't doing the same thing.

That was it! I suddenly had the answer to my happiness, and I found that answer in forgiveness. I had to forgive my former friend. I had to forgive myself, and once I arrived at that stage, I was finally able to forgive her of what I perceived to be a direct violation of our friendship.

I want you to pay close attention to what I said. I repeat, "I forgave her of what I perceived to be a direct violation of our friendship." Not only did I forgive her, I met with her one-on-one, and we discussed our individual viewpoints on the incidents.

I did not become her friend again, or at least not right away. I took baby steps rebuilding my communication with her, but at least I was taking steps forward. After constantly practicing forgiveness (and believe me, in order to forgive, you have to practice forgiveness) through my actions and words, I moved to a point where I could be in the midst of her company and not feel any anger or resentment. I finally felt at peace.

*"The process of forgiveness is not going to be easy."*

The process of forgiveness is not going to be easy. It is the most important stage, and the most challenging stage. You cannot be afraid to let go of that security blanket of bitterness and anger. This stage in the process of transformation requires you to be vulnerable. Forgiveness does not come overnight, but it is achievable with daily practice.

### It's Time to Do the Work!

I want YOU to begin the process of forgiveness. Let's start by writing a letter to the one who hurt you. If you need to forgive yourself, address the letter to yourself. In this letter, I want you to describe your viewpoint. Describe your feelings of hurt. Explain how your hurt was caused by the other person's actions, or maybe by your own actions. At the end of this letter, I want you to write THREE words. Write these three words in all CAPS, "I FORGIVE YOU" and then list all the things that you are committed to forgiving.

Once you are done writing this letter, I want you to read it daily. You don't have to give this letter to the person that hurt you. Maybe you are forgiving yourself, but nonetheless, I want you to read this letter daily. I want you to read it every day until you begin to feel the power of forgiveness. Some of you who are reading this book may be clinicians and, if so, before trying this exercise with your clients, please assess their level of readiness.

*Chapter Six*

# Stage Four: CLEARING

You may ask, "What is clearing?" "What does it all mean?" Well before I answer your questions, let us first examine what is meant by the word *clear*. According to the Miriam-Webster Dictionary, "clear" means bright and luminous, cloudless, free from mist, haze and dust, or untroubled; serene. Another definition says clean and pure, free from blemishes, easily seen through, or transparent.

I want to focus on one particular section in the definition of clear. "*Untroubled.*" When you are emotionally hurt, whether you are depressed, angry, traumatized, or numb, or you have an unforgiving spirit, you will more than likely stay stuck in your misery, and everyone around you will notice just how miserable you truly are. This will show up in multiple ways.

*"Hurtful words plague your thinking, and take control over your life."*

One way your misery will show up is when you are repeatedly bothered by the words of the past, and those words still have power in your life, and rent space in your head. You further reinforce hurtful words by replaying them over and over in your mind. Hurtful words like: "You're stupid." "You're fat." "You're ugly." "You'll never amount to anything." "You're damaged goods." "No one will want you." "I don't love you anymore." The list of hurtful words are plentiful. Misery allows hurtful words to plague your thinking, and take control over your life.

Living in misery makes it easy to recall the times when you were violated, abused, beaten, betrayed, and abandoned. Misery makes it easy to remember the mistakes you made in your past. Misery doesn't allow you to heal. It keeps you stuck and haunted. If you ever struggled with drugs, alcohol, or promiscuity, misery will remind you of all your wrong doings. It is common to remember the day you were raped and taken advantage of, but misery will make you believe it was all your fault. All of these events will get programmed into your thinking, and it eventually becomes the fuel for your depression, anger, resentment, and unforgiving spirit.

Clearing simply means you commit to releasing the behaviors, negative beliefs, and people that no longer serve you. Clearing allows you to dismiss negative beliefs and thoughts, you become *Untroubled*. This is what the fourth stage is about. It is about clearing your mind of negative thoughts and beliefs. This is the stage where you start the process of dismantling those damaging thoughts, and replacing them with empowering thoughts and happy memories.

Let me get one thing straight, clearing is not fooling yourself into believing that having a new way of thinking means you have been changed. This is a common mistake that many people make. They absorb a lot of information on improving their lives and changing their thinking, but they never apply it correctly—there seems to be a disconnect in the transfer of learning (TOL). For whatever reason, it becomes difficult to transfer the learned information into action. I know this to be true because the behaviors of miserable people doesn't change, and they continue to hold onto people, places, and things that no longer serve them.

I have worked with plenty of people who appears as if they have made progress in their lives. In conversations, they can repeat all the things they have learned about changing their thinking. They speak positivity, but their actions and behavior scream negativity. Over the years, I have learned to pay attention, and listen closely.

When TOL has not occurred, miserable people will harbor anger and resentment. They show signs of depression, they have an unforgiving spirit, and the list goes on. The worst, and probably most damaging, is when they keep the same circle of friends and/or family that add-on to their misery. These friends and family members are energy zappers, and emotionally draining.

Clearing is having the courage to remove yourself from all negativity. This includes people, places, and things, and family members are not exempt. If you can relate to what I am saying, and have not been successful in the clearing process, or if you find yourself constantly reverting back to those taunting thoughts, it may simply mean you need to go back and work on the first, second, and third stages of the transformation process.

> ***"Clearing is having the courage to remove yourself from all negativity."***

If you do not master the stages of Acceptance, Awareness, and Forgiveness, you are not ready to clear your head of negative thoughts and feelings, and you will continue to attract like-minded people that will reinforce your misery. Clearing is such a powerful stage because, if done correctly, it completely transforms your life. You will experience such a breakthrough like never before.

To put it all into perspective, let me familiarize you to one of God's most significant creatures here on earth. Are you familiar with the life of a caterpillar? The caterpillar is an interesting insect to me because its life cycle resembles much of the life that many of us have gone through.

First, the caterpillar doesn't get to choose where it will be born. It doesn't get to choose if it will be born rich or poor, if it will be abused or loved, abandoned or nurtured. A caterpillar doesn't get to choose its life's path. Whatever plant or leaf the caterpillar is born on, that is where he or she will eat. This is the caterpillar's start to survival. As the caterpillar eats, it begins to grow, and at each growth spurt, the caterpillar molts — it sheds its outgrown skin.

# TTRANSFORMING PAIN INTO POSSIBILITY: A PRACTICAL APPROACH

### *"Before transforming, the caterpillar did not have wings."*

Once the caterpillar has grown as much as it can, it then forms into a pupa. The pupa is the cocoon-like protection that keeps the caterpillar safe during the transformation process, it protects the caterpillar as it begins to morph into something beautiful. This is the stage where there caterpillar is most vulnerable, and has to trust in the process as it undergoes a remarkable transformation. Although the pupa seems motionless and untroubled, major changes are happening that the outside world is not privy to witness.

The final stage is where the full butterfly emerges. Before transforming, the caterpillar did not have wings. Once transformation is complete, the caterpillar not only has wings, but it usually has a beautiful design and vivid colors.

None of us, and I truly mean NONE OF US, had the opportunity to choose where and when we were born. Like the caterpillar, we simply lived the life we were dealt, and we are all sure to have stories of unpleasant beginnings and experiences. No matter what, like the caterpillar, you will grow through your experiences, shedding your old skin, and, at every stage of development, you will have a new experience. It is important to know that your pupa stage, when you are wrapped in a cocoon, is your personal journey. Others don't need to know your inner thoughts and feelings, nor will they understand you. If you are not careful, and you share your thoughts, plans, feelings, and experiences, people will offer you advice based off their own narrative. Their story is not your story. You have to allow yourself to undergo a quiet transformation, and trust the process.

Eventually, a major transformation will occur. You will eventually morph into something different than what you started as. One thing is certain, you will not always be a caterpillar. What will you morph into? Will you be a butterfly, admired by many? Or will you be a moth, unsightly and unpleasant? You get to decide.

### It's Time to Do the Work!

Take this journey with me. I dare you to live like the caterpillar. It's time to accept the life you were dealt. It's time to pinpoint the root cause of your pain, and raise your awareness. It's time to release yourself from depression, anger, and fear. Start this process by forgiving your mother and father, your husband or wife, your friends and associates for the hurts you experienced. It's time to transform your life by renewing your mind.

Go to a quiet place and be prepared to be honest with yourself. On a lined sheet of paper, I want you to make a crease down the middle. On the left side of the paper, list the names of individuals who do not add value to your life. The names should include people who do not encourage or support you. It should include names of people who drain you emotionally and mentally. It should be people who are critical and judgmental, as well as people who entice you to engage in negative activities and bad behaviors.

On the right side of the paper, and corresponding to each

name that was written down on the left, write what action step you are willing to take TODAY to clear them from your life. This won't be easy and may require baby steps. Action steps can include limiting telephone conversations and text messages. It can include deleting them as friends on social media platforms. It can be a phone call to express your feelings of hurt, and give notice of the end of the relationship or friendship. It can be turning down offers, or saying NO more often than not. I want you to read this list daily, and take daily action steps toward your goal of clearing people, places, and things that no longer serve you.

*Chapter Seven*

# Stage Five: MANIFESTATION

The last stage in the transformation process is the opportunity to have a fresh start. By now, you have committed to conquering your pain, and transforming your life. By now, you should have taken steps in the forgiveness process, and you should have started clearing negative people, places, and things from your life.

***"It is necessary for you to think big and act successful."***

Manifestation is the stage where you start to bring your vision for your life into perspective. This is a time when you get to re-tell your life story from a different perspective, a different point of view. This stage is so important because it allows you to write a new truth, and YOU get to play the lead part. You can no longer play it small. It is necessary for you to think big and act successful.

Often times, we program our minds into believing the lies that have been said about us and, even worse, we believe things about our past that keep us immobile and paralyzed. The lies we tell ourselves, and believe, are not meant to empower. Instead of motivating us, they tear us down, affect our thought processes, and ultimately stop us from living the lives we are destined to live.

As a child or adolescent, if you were told that you were ugly and unattractive, you probably spent most of your life trying to make yourself beautiful. Some of you wear make-up each and every day to hide what you believe is "bad skin" or imperfections. Some people go as far as engaging in cosmetic surgery to hide their imperfections.

For example, if you were told your feet were not pretty, I am willing to bet that you go out of your way to keep your feet covered. Even in the summer, when you are hot, and want to be comfortable in sandals, you choose to hide your feet because somebody, in the past, said your feet were ugly. As a result of someone's opinion, you wear closed-toe sandals and shoes, or sneakers despite how hot and uncomfortable they are in the summer months. You simply refuse to show your feet because of a negative comment you received.

### *"Time heals all wounds, but you have to stop picking at the scabs."*

One of the greatest atrocities committed against the self is emotional, verbal, and physical abuse by a loved one. Repeated exposure of abuse will erode the self-esteem, self-confidence, and the identity of self. Subjection to a constant barrage of negative statements will eventually cause you to believe them as true. Being told you are dumb, sloppy, fat, poor, or ugly (to name a few), will rent space in your head, and occupy your thinking. Some of you believe no one wants you, no one loves you, and you aren't worthy of happiness. These hurtful lies that you believe have disempowered your life, and led you to the road of destruction.

Completing the first four stages is the prerequisite to the 5th and final stage in the transformation process. It is your opportunity to find a new truth in what was once believed to be your life story. You cannot change what happened in your past, but you can change how you feel. You can change what you believe about yourself. You no longer have to live life constantly recovering from your past hurts. You no longer have to live life walking around with a wounded heart, believing it is incapable of healing. Time heals all wounds, but you have to stop picking at the scabs.

Manifestation is about telling a new story. It is not about forgetting your past, or erasing your memory. It is about standing on your story, using it as a testimony, and a stepping stone, for creating powerful outcomes. It is about stating the facts, but controlling the future. Let me put it to you in the simplest form. You cannot change the fact that you were abused, bullied, ridiculed, beaten, raped, or had fallen victim to the streets. However, you can change what you believe about who you are, and you can change your future.

*"Manifestation is about telling a new story."*

This reminds me of my childhood. I am going to share a

little bit about myself, which I ordinarily do not do. I was born to a single mother, who was never married, and I never had a relationship with my father. I don't remember how he looked, and I barely remember any of our minimum interactions. I vividly remember growing up poor — very poor, but I did not comprehend what it meant to be poor because of my mother's ability to shield both my brother and I from its effects.

As a young girl, probably around the age of four, my mother, brother, and I lost our apartment, forcing us to move in the middle of the night. There was no preparation or warning. I remember playing outside, one day, and the next day I was in a totally new neighborhood. Completely tired, and virtually unable to walk up six flights of stairs, my mother knocked on an apartment door, holding me in her arms, and my brother stood by her side, calm and poised. An older looking woman open the door, mumbled something to my mother, and walked away as we begin to file into the apartment. I later came to realize we moved into my great grandmother's house in the middle of the night, with nothing but clothes inside garbage bags.

It would have been no big deal if my great grandmother's apartment had multiple bedrooms, but it did not. She only had one bedroom that housed my cousin, my great aunt, who is mentally retarded, and my great grandmother. I remember having to sleep in the living room on a "Roll Away Bed" with my mother, and my brother slept on the couch. In the bedroom, my cousin, great aunt, and great grandmother slept.

When my great grandmother passed away, years later, we remained in that same apartment with the same people—my mother, brother, cousin, great aunt, and I. As you could imagine, money was tight and almost nonexistent. Growing up, I was no stranger to welfare. I was no stranger to living in the dark—without electricity, having no phone, and having to borrow items such as rice, sugar, syrup, and other things most people usually don't intend on giving back. I am not ashamed to share this story as an adult because this was my life.

> *"To add insult to injury, the words I LOVE YOU were far and few between."*

It was a life of poverty. In addition to being dirt poor, my mother's idea method of discipline was an extension cord, a shoe, a broomstick, or a belt, if I was lucky. It was rough growing up in my household. To add insult to injury, as a child, the words, 'I LOVE YOU' were few and far between. Affection was not the norm in my household growing up, and the lack of affection played a major part in how I viewed myself as a young adult.

I measured my mother's love by the things she bought me, and the activities she somehow paid for me to participate in, such as dance school, swimming, softball, and volley ball. I don't know how she got the money to get my uniforms, and other items that I needed, but she did, and that's how I measured her love. Our relationship was unique. We had a very, very inimitable relationship. I wouldn't say our relationship was bad, it was just different. Despite my life circumstances, and despite my environment, my mother always believed in me. The problem was that no one else did.

### *"Every day felt like a battlefield."*

I was made fun of all through my youth. The guys teased me about my "knock knees." Girls made fun of my hair. I was called names like, "Blackie" and "Tar Baby." I was teased because I had to use food stamps to buy items from the store. I was fatter than the other little girls in my dance school, and I had crooked bottom teeth.

If it wasn't one thing, it was another. As I got older, from childhood to adolescence, it got worse. The ridicule and judgment did not come only from children. Believe it or not, it came from adults and family members as well. It made me feel inferior as though I was not good enough.

Every day felt like a battlefield. If I was not physically fighting the kids who taunted me, I was fighting the adults who made fun of me. The ones who told me I was not good enough or smart enough. The ones who told me I would not be successful, and I would not make it. I spent all of my youth and adolescence fighting. I started to develop a sense of failure, and a belief that people who are like me just don't make it in life. They simply don't do great things.

I was living a life of self-defeating thoughts and limiting beliefs, but something shifted when I was about 16 years old (I will never forget this day, I remember it as though it were yesterday). My aunt was my role model. She was the most beautiful woman, inside and out. She was strong, independent, and adventurous. Being around her made me feel confident and secure. At every opportunity, she would teach me how to love myself, and how to take care of myself. She would correct my behavior, and kindly remind me how a lady ought to act. She reminded her daughter and nieces, including me, that it is important, as a woman, to be able to take care of yourself. I couldn't argue with that. I witnessed her practicing what she preached.

My world came crashing down when she died unexpectedly from pneumonia. At the time, it was called "walking pneumonia." My aunt didn't know she was sick. Her death literally ripped me apart, and I spent years stitching myself back up, one day at a time. With her death, I knew I had to make it. I had to succeed. I had to pick up where she left off. I started to tell myself that I was meant to live a full life.

I took a chance on life and, most importantly, I took a chance on myself. I started the process of turning my life around. I changed the way I thought about myself. I changed the way I thought about other people. I started to realize, and I started to believe "I am beautiful and I am smart." I began to believe that there were people in my life that can help me achieve greatness, and fulfill my ultimate destiny.

> *"I stopped living life to make other people happy and started living a life of happiness."*

I began to speak with conviction as though I was already living the life of my dreams. Instead of lashing out at people and getting an attitude, or making excuses for my upbringing, I would say things like, "I can't wait until I graduate college," or "One day I am going to own my own business." I became clear on what I wanted to achieve. Whenever the opportunity presented itself, I would speak about getting a "good job," and returning to my neighborhood to help others. My whole thought process shifted. I no longer focused on dressing up to feel beautiful. I no longer focused on my weight, or trying to walk without signs of being knock-kneed. I stopped living life to make other people happy, and I started living a life of happiness. This didn't happen overnight. It was a process, but each day it got easier. It became second nature.

## It's Time to Do the Work!

Are you living out your dreams? Are you ready to tell a new story about who you are? Now is the time for you to take control of your future. It's time to start living the life you want and deserve. It's no longer about who you used to be. It's about who you are. You are beautiful. You are smart. You are entitled to be happy. You are exactly what you want to be. NO EXCEPTIONS!

Take a few days to think about how you want your life to be. Do you want to be a school teacher, a doctor, or a lawyer? Do you want to be debt-free and financially independent? Maybe you want to end a bad relationship or, just the opposite, get married. After you determine your vision for your life, I want you to write it down followed by a list of action steps you must take in order to accomplish your goals. Give yourself a completion date. Be realistic with your goals and timeframes. Put your list in a visual place, and review it daily.

Follow through on your goals. Obtain an accountability partner who will commit to meeting with you bi-weekly or monthly. Someone you can trust with your vision. If there is no one you know with whom you can talk one-on-one, join a Facebook group that consists of like-minded individuals all working toward their goals and visions. Find a skilled therapist that can help you move through the pain and into possibility. Get a mentor, or a coach. Do something, just don't sit idle.

*Chapter Eight*

# HATERS, SCAVENGERS, and COPYCATS

Transformation seldom comes without challenges. There will be a time when you are going to feel like people are not supporters of your vision and your dreams. Although it will hurt, and you might get upset, you need to remain focused on your goals. It's inevitable. No matter where you go, you are always going to pick up one of three types of people, and some of you will pick up all three. You will either pick up a HATER, a SCAVENGER, or a COPYCAT.

> **"The hater is the one that will notice your transformation, yet feel the need to remind you how you used to be."**

You are probably familiar with the term *hater*. You've seen the term on t-shirts, or read the term on social media. The term became most popular when Katt Williams, a popular comedian, addressed it in his standup comedy performance titled, *Pimp Chronicles*. The *hater* is someone who never wants to see you do well in life. A hater is one who is a critic, and is probably not successful in her own endeavors. At every moment, she shares her opinions and ideas for how she thinks you should live your life, and pursue your dreams. A *hater* will show up at your house just to see how you're living so she can talk about you to others who are haters as well. The *hater* is the one that will tell you she is going to support you in your dreams, or be there for you, but when you need her, she is never around. A *hater* doesn't have to be a friend, a *hater* can be a family member. Just because family members are related to you, it doesn't mean they support you in all your endeavors or ventures.

The *hater* is the one who will notice your transformation, yet feel the need to remind you how you used to be. Share your idea with a *hater,* and she will tell you that your idea doesn't make any sense. A *hater* may not verbally tell you your dream is too big, but that is exactly how she will make you feel. A hater is skillful in making you feel like you are being ridiculous and unrealistic. Rest assured - a *hater's* only job is to hate. Don't waste your time trying to get a hater to be more positive and supportive of you.

The *scavenger* is a person who always wants your leftover items and ideas. Some *scavengers* even want your leftover relationships. A scavenger's plan is to always use your items, ideas, or past relationships so she can incorporate them into her own ideas or lifestyle. The *scavenger* may present as a "go getter," but she is not invested in her own success. She is not invested in doing the work. A scavenger builds her image from the stuff you have discarded, or from ideas of yours that you didn't bring to life.

> *"Scavengers are ready and available to eat whatever is leftover, or not being used."*

A person with these characteristics is similar to scavengers at the bottom of the sea, or in the wild. Scavengers at the bottom of the sea eat decomposed and dead organisms. Scavengers in the wild eat dead animals. They are not predators. They don't do the work of hunting for their survival. Scavengers are ready and available to eat whatever is leftover, or not being used.

For example, suppose you organized an event. At your event, the décor caught everyone's attention as it was the highlight of the evening. The s*cavenger* is the one who comes up to you at the end of your event, showers you with compliments, and immediately asks to borrow your items. It was your event that gave her ideas. She now has an idea to host her own event, and invite her network, BUT she plans to use your materials to bring her idea to life. She has no plans of buying her own items, or her own decorations. She intends to use what she thinks you will no longer use. While on your journey of transformation, it is your job to be aware of this type of behavior, and to learn to address it at its root. I am not asking you to be mean because being mean will only block your blessings. What I am asking is that you know the type of people that are in your circle.

> *"These people are the ones you call family and friends, but will turn around and stab you in the back when you least expect it."*

The *copycat* is pretty much self-explanatory. The *copycat* is the person who copies everything you do. For example, imagine you worked hard all year. To celebrate your success and accomplishments, you purchase a car. Feeling excited, you call your friend unaware that she is a copycat (or maybe you are aware), and you share your joy of purchasing a new car. She gets excited with you, and wants to come over to inspect your new vehicle. She is more than happy for you, and is filled with compliments. She presents in a genuine manner and expresses her happiness for you. Suddenly, the conversation shifts, and she expresses her thoughts of purchasing a new car as well. Before you know it, she decides to purchase the same exact car as yours, or she tries to top your car by purchasing a more expensive vehicle with all the bells and whistles. When you share your thoughts, ideas, and vision with a *copycat*, she will present as your biggest cheerleader and immediately express that she shared the same thoughts and ideas. Not only does she tell you your idea is great, she turns around and does the same exact thing that you shared with her.

You have to be careful with these types of people. They are energy zappers, and are known to rent space in your head. These people are the ones you call *family* and *friends,* but will turn around and stab you in the back when you least expect it. Associating with them will throw you off track, and cause you to fall back into your negative thinking and behavior.

Not everyone is going to share your vision or your dreams. Not everyone is going to want to see you succeed. Not everyone is going to want you to exceed her in life even if she is not doing anything with her own life. Be cautious and careful when around energy zappers, but don't spend too much time thinking about them. You cannot afford to lose your focus or hope. You have to remain steadfast and remain on your path.

Don't pay attention to the *haters*. That is what they are here to do. They are simply here to hate. Let them hate.

Don't pay attention to the *scavengers*. You control what you will and will not give them. My suggestion is to utilize the power of the word "No." You don't have to give the *scavengers* whatever they ask for just because they are "cool" with you.

As for the *copycats*, the minute they copy you once, they will copy you always. Learn to keep your visions, your dreams, and your goals to yourself. You don't want to run the risk of inviting a *copycat* to steal your ideas. Once you notice the signs of a *copycat*, you have to commit to writing your dreams, ideas, and visions on paper, and only talk about them <u>after</u> you have accomplished them. This way, it will become your testimony.

> **"Remain focused with your blinders on as you march ahead pursuing your dreams."**

As you move forward in this journey, know that you have a purpose. You must get on the path of transformation so that you can become a better you. A better you does not need confirmation and validation from others. You must have faith that you are going to reach your destination. Remain focused with your blinders on as you march ahead pursuing your dreams. I am not promising that this journey will be easy. I want you to know that there will be setbacks and failures. There is only one thing for certain - you are destined to be a success.

*Chapter Nine*

# STAYING THE COURSE

Making positive changes in your life is not an easy process. Not only will you attract people who do not genuinely support you in your transformation process, but you yourself will battle your own thoughts, fears, doubts, and negative behaviors. Becoming a better person requires commitment, dedication, and determination. These requirements may seem easy, but I assure you that unless you apply all three, you will find yourself drifting off track, and relapsing into negative thoughts, behaviors, and associates.

> *"When you commit to the process of transformation, you take daily actions and steps to progress forward."*

Before you make a commitment to transform your life, you have to have an understanding of "WHY" you want to change your life. Being able to answer the question of "why" will allow you to put things into perspective. It will help you create a clear vision and develop a plan.

Why would you want to change to become a better person? Maybe your current situation no longer serves a purpose or benefits you. It's possible that you may have lost some valuable people in your life. Have you been pushing people away, and now find that you are alone? Is your attitude and behavior affecting you at work? Do you feel that people find it difficult to socialize with you?

No matter the reason, if you are not sure of why you want to change, you will never commit to the process of transformation.

**Remember: It is not about who you used to be, but all about who you are and who you are becoming.**

Commitment means you make a decision to be loyal to the process. It is a promise you make to yourself to stay the course in order to accomplish your goals when it seems difficult. When you commit to the process of transformation, you take daily actions and steps to progress forward. You walk boldly, knowing you are in control of your own thoughts and behaviors, maintaining the belief that change is possible.

Commitment to change is not easy, partly because internal and external forces will always remind you of who you used to be. Don't be discouraged when faced with this dilemma. Remember: It is not about who you used to be, but all about who you are and who you are becoming.

In addition to commitment, you have to be dedicated. Dedication is a self-sacrificing devotion. You must be willing to dedicate all your time and attention to the process. This means a constant reconditioning of your thoughts by immersing yourself in information, seminars, workshops, and other settings that allow you to learn a new way of being. Often times, people shy away from trying new things because they fear being judged, ridiculed, or misunderstood. Do not expect to change if you are not willing to learn new things and to meet new people.

Change requires you to step out of your comfort zone. This will automatically cause you to question your confidence level. Remaining in your comfort zone keeps you in a place of complacency. It limits your beliefs, and it leads you to believe that you are not able to change. All too often I hear people say, "I am too old to change." This belief system will keep you in your same condition, continuously struggling with your emotions. Dedicating yourself to change will work to produce greater outcomes beyond your imagination.

> *"Remaining in your comfort zone keeps you in a place of complacency."*

If you have ever tried to lose weight, tone up, or gain muscle, you know it is not an overnight process. You not only have to be committed and dedicated to the process, you have to be determined to achieve results. Determination is not giving up. When you are determined, you will go the extra mile even when you are tired, upset, uncertain, or afraid. Determination requires you to be willing to put yourself out on the line.

Determination overcomes all obstacles. Determination is that inner drive that gives you supernatural strength and power to keep going even when your tank is on empty. You have to be determined to make it despite your barriers. You have to be totally focused even if it means losing some friends and associates. When you are determined, you are able to turn the doubts and criticism of others into motivation. Success is no longer an option, it is the only way. You can't be afraid to fail or make a mistake. It is all part of the process.

Determination overrides fear. Determination causes you to be bold and brave. A determined spirit attracts the attention of others. You will become a topic of interest and you will unintentionally recruit fans. People will want to emulate your progress and success. Determination is the ingredient that fuels hope and sustains the mental energy needed to succeed.

*Chapter Ten*

# TEAMWORK MAKES THE DREAM WORK

By now, I hope you have made a commitment to start transforming your pain into possibility. Getting started may seem easy and, for some, it is easy.

> **No matter who you decide to work with, don't take this journey alone.**

I don't want you to make the mistake of going through this process alone. I know many women who believed they did not need help transforming their lives. They did not see the benefit of engaging others through the process. I highly recommend building a team of support while you take a journey into wellness. Some team members might include therapists, licensed clinicians, psychologists, counselors, mentors, or coaches. No matter who you decide to work with, don't take this journey alone.

## *Therapist*

A therapist is usually someone who is skilled in psychological methods to help people work through psychological problems and challenges. There are many types of therapists skilled in different disciplines. Some therapists specifically work with families and married couples. Other therapists may incorporate a variety of treatment methods to help individuals achieve their goals. It is important to engage a therapist who can help you to get your desired results, and develop the needed skills so in the future you can combat problems on your own.

A therapist is most likely to hold a master's degree, and may have received post-graduate training. In order to practice their trade, therapists must be licensed by their state licensing board. In addition to meeting the educational and licensure requirements, therapists are required to complete continuing education credits in order to keep their licenses active and current.

Don't be fooled. Regardless of their education and training, not all therapists are created equal. It is important to build rapport and trust with a therapist, or the process of therapy will be counterproductive. A therapist is better known as a change agent. A therapist works to help you transform your life. An ideal therapist will be able to help you change the way you think and respond to some of life's unexpected challenges.

## Licensed Clinicians

A licensed clinician can be a professional counselor, social worker, marriage and family therapist, or alcohol and drug counselor. Just like therapists, licensed clinicians hold master's degrees in their respective disciplines. Also, licensed clinicians most likely received supervised training by a licensed clinical supervisor, and completed a specific number of clinical hours in order to satisfy the state licensing requirements. Lastly, licensed clinicians are legally able to operate an independent practice without ongoing, mandated supervision. Just like therapists, licensed clinicians must maintain annual continuing education credits to keep their licenses active and current.

Licensed clinicians provide a variety of services to help people experiencing disorders such as depression, anxiety, stress, workplace issues, family problems, relationship issues, or issues related to abuse. People who seek services of licensed clinicians generally are in need of psychotherapy, group therapy, evaluations, drug and alcohol assessments, and patient education. Currently, the only master's level clinician that can prescribe medication is a nurse practitioner.

## *Psychologists*

Licensed psychologists provide many of the same services as master's level clinicians. Some psychologists have a specialty, while others may be a general practitioner. In addition to psychotherapy, group therapy, evaluations, drug and alcohol assessments, and patient education services, psychologists may also administer and interpret psychological tests, such as IQ, personality or behavioral tests.

Psychologists who provide clinical services (as in the services named above) must have a doctoral degree. This is usually recognized by the credentials that follow their name such as Ph.D, Psy.D or Ed.D. Very similar to clinicians, psychologists must complete a supervised internship providing psychological services in a clinical setting, and maintain continuing education credits to keep their licenses current and active (this varies by state).

*Counselors*

I want to make extremely clear that there is a big difference between being a professional counselor in comparison to someone who provides counseling services by virtue of his or her skills or assigned role (i.e. church clergy, friend, colleague, or unlicensed individual). A professional counselor has both the education and training to provide counseling services which includes talk therapy and group therapy, diagnosis, assessments, and evaluations. Professional counselors are least likely to approach counseling from a psychodynamic approach (digging into the past) and usually take a more humanistic approach (client-centered therapy).

Professional counselors hold a master's degree, complete supervised training, and have to pass a board examination in order to obtain a license to practice. Unlicensed counselors are not regulated by a governing board and may not have had proper training. There are many lay people who use the term "counselor" who have not had the training, or the necessary education to competently practice the skill set. Going to a religious counselor who does not have the education and training may or may not be the right choice for you when your problem extends beyond issues with your faith.

## Mentors

A mentor is a person who is experienced in a particular field, or with life experiences, who guides a less experienced person. A mentor is a person who is trustworthy, dependable, and who exhibits positive behavior. In order for a mentor to be effective, he or she must be available, authentic, and engaged in the process.

Unlike a therapist, licensed clinician, psychologist, or counselor, a mentor usually works with people on a volunteer basis. When choosing a mentor, be sure the mentor is committed to your personal and/or professional development. When money is removed from the equation, the support and counsel of a mentor should be of genuine concern. A mentor is vested in your future. The relationship with a mentor should be longstanding.

## Coaches

The term "coach" is gaining popularity at a rapid rate. Coaches assist people to reach their goals by strategizing and planning with a laser-sharp focus. A coach provides the individual with the tools and structure needed to accomplish a specific goal. A coach will hold an individual accountable for moving her goals forward. In coaching, it is necessary to help the individual reframe her belief system. A coach brings awareness to those challenging areas that keep the individual from making progress.

Good coaches are known by the results they have produced for others. When seeking coaching services, it is important to define what type of coach will best suit your needs. There are several types of coaches available. Some examples are life coaches, business coaches, executive coaches, and relationship coaches.

It may be enticing to select a friend to be your coach, but this isn't something I would recommend. A professional coach maintains objectivity and distance that helps maintain the necessary boundaries within the relationship. It is also important for the coach to maintain a high level of confidentiality. You may need to share sensitive information in order for the coach to address issues that may be blocking progress.

## *Getting Started*

Now that you have a clearer picture of the different types of supports available to you, it's time to make a decision to move forward. No matter what type of member(s) you select to be on your transformation team, you have to do your research to get the right fit for you. Ask other people you trust, get referrals from trusted sources, and search the Internet and/or social media before making a final decision. Make sure whoever you select is an authentic person.

It may take more than one try to assemble your transformation team, but don't be discouraged, and don't quit. As long as you stay committed to the process you will be successful. Don't focus on cost, or the length of time it may take. Staying the course should be your primary goal. You must trust that you will get everything you set out to achieve.

If making a commitment to a therapist, mentor, or coach is not something you are readily comfortable doing, start by attending workshops and seminars that are focused on helping persons transform their pain into possibility. Something about a presenter may "click" with you, and you may find yourself with a possible member for your transformation team.

*It is your time to shine.*

*It is your time to live free.*

I hope you enjoyed reading this book. I hope you are ready to release yourself of your past. I hope you are excited about freeing yourself from the mental bondage that has stopped you from living your best life ever. It is your time to shine. It is your time to live free.

For more information or to obtain services offered by The Center for Counseling and Holistic Services, please visit our website at www.njcchs.org or email us at info@njcchs.org.

# AFTERWORD

It is important to note that IRIS was not created in a vacuum. There are many contributing members in the field of mental health and psychotherapy who spent countless years studying the thought process and behaviors of multiple populations. In providing treatment for persons who are experiencing increased stress, depression, anxiety, and other mental health illnesses and disorders, it is important to consider practices that are evidence-based. The human mind is particularly vulnerable and fragile and we must be socially and psychologically responsible when providing treatment.

Evidence-based practice is all about measurable outcomes. It is the use of systematic decision-making processes. No longer can psychotherapists rely on instincts and "gut reactions" when they provide treatment. Scientific evidence puts credence into our work as psychotherapists and mental health workers. Evidence-based practice is about offering treatments and interventions that are effective, taking into account the risks associated with the practices.

IRIS is a 5-stage strategy designed to help women who have experienced some of life's greatest challenges. IRIS is based upon some well-known, proven and effective modalities. IRIS incorporates Acceptance Commitment Therapy (ACT),

Mindfulness, the REACH treatment method on forgiveness, Cognitive Behavioral Therapy (CBT), and Solution Focused Therapy (SFT). Each known treatment method has proven to be successful in numerous clinical trials and research. Each method has its place in the IRIS strategy, and can be used interchangeably, given the individual client and her treatment needs.

## Acceptance Commitment Therapy

Acceptance Commitment Therapy, better known as ACT, was developed in the 1980's by Steven C. Hayes, Kelly G. Wilson and Kirk Strostahl. ACT is a widely used treatment method designed to help people with a broad range of disorders. ACT is reported to work well with those who suffer from depression. ACT mainly works to change the relationship a person has with her own thoughts, feelings, memories, and emotions. It is more than being aware, although awareness is part of the process. ACT is an action-oriented treatment method. Psychotherapists applying this method work with an individual in order to make a commitment to changing her behavior by becoming aware of how her thoughts affect her behavior and mood.

ACT works well in the acceptance stage of IRIS. In this stage, the psychotherapist helps the client to accept things as they are—in the here and now. The psychotherapist helps the client become aware of her negative thought patterns and how those thought patterns influence her behavior and affect her moods.

The first stage of IRIS is more about taking the client off autopilot, thereby causing her to manage her thoughts and moods more effectively.

It is easy to automatically allow thoughts to invade one's mind without giving them much thought. This is a human thing to do. When there is a disorder or disease present in the mind, negative thinking can become deeply rooted in a person's psyche. As the saying goes, "The mind is a terrible thing to waste." Achieving acceptance allows the client to focus on her thoughts and behaviors, and ultimately make a commitment to change them.

## *Mindfulness*

Many people live their lives on autopilot. People are reactive to their environment and, without knowing, they often find comfort in playing the role of the victim. Being a victim can be a comfortable place. When one is a victim, one receives comfort while any blame is shifted. When people are unaware of why things happen, and unaware of their emotions and behavior patterns, they fail to exercise the skills necessary to initiate change.

Mindfulness, a centuries old practice that is deeply rooted in Eastern culture and Buddhism, is a powerful therapeutic technique. Mindfulness is more than just being aware. Mindfulness is about observing one's life in the moment by becoming aware of one's thoughts, feelings, and moods, then taking an active approach to informed decision making.

Jon Kabat-Zinn, who founded the Center for Mindfulness in

Medicine, Health Care, and Society at the University of Massachusetts Medical School, defines Mindfulness as: "Paying attention in a particular way: on purpose, in the present moment, and non-judgmentally." I like to describe Mindfulness as a "Think before you speak and act" approach. For someone to be able to sit in her discomfort and assess the current situation from a nonjudgmental mindset, Mindfulness can help a great deal to relieve stress, depression, and anxiety, as well as to manage her moods.

What I find most powerful with mindfulness is the ability to help a person move forward from past hurt and pain. A person cannot change her past, but she can change the course of her future. Living in the past, and worrying about things that cannot be changed, is counterproductive to living a full life. When a person lives in the here and now, she commits to taking the lead in her life's story.

## REACH Method for Forgiveness

Forgiveness is one of the most difficult things to achieve because people truly misunderstand the concept of forgiveness. When someone who has been wronged (or is directly connected to someone who was wronged) hears the term forgiveness, she almost always associates it with one or more of the following:

- Reconciliation
- Forgetting
- Excusing or overlooking the act

Forgiveness is something entirely different. It is a powerful choice one makes that can lead to greater well-being, peace of mind, and better relationships. Forgiveness requires a shift in thinking. Forgiveness is decreasing or eliminating negative thoughts and emotions toward a person (or persons) who may have wronged you. Forgiveness is not something that happens overnight. Often times, a person is unaware of the hurt and pain she carries around with her each day. When she is confronted, it is not uncommon for a person to deny her pain. Even when she admits to her negative emotions, anger, and bitterness, she is unaware that these emotions are due to a lack of forgiveness on her part.

The REACH method of forgiveness was developed by Dr. Everett L. Worthington Jr., a professor of Counseling Psychology at Virginia Commonwealth University. He is a pioneer researcher in the field of forgiveness, and constructed the 5-step REACH model to facilitate the process of forgiveness.

REACH is an acronym that stands for the following:

- Recall the hurt
- Empathize with the one who hurt you
- Altruistic gift of forgiveness
- Commitment to forgive
- Hold on to the forgiveness

The REACH method is a powerful approach to reaching forgiveness because it not only retrains the brain to think differently from the victim's standpoint, but it helps the victim empathize with the offender. The REACH method does not offer reconciliation with the offender. It simply helps the victim free herself from the imprisonment of a negative, vengeful mind.

## Cognitive Behavioral Therapy

Cognitive Behavioral Therapy, pioneered by Dr. Aaron T, Beck in the 1960's, is a helpful tool for individuals to become aware of inaccurate and/or negative thinking. Helping to identify negative and inaccurate thoughts allows for a more objective and healthy response. When a person is able to view challenging situations from multiple perspectives, she reduces reactive behavior. The goal of using CBT within the IRIS model is to help participants respond to life's mishaps more effectively.

CBT is a hands-on practical approach to treatment. CBT is more than talk therapy. It includes formulating a strategy to help the participant tackle unwarranted thoughts, beliefs, and feelings. CBT is goal oriented and allows for measurable results. I believe if a person wants her life to be different, she has to be active in the process of change. A person can talk until she is blue in the face, but unless she makes a commitment to change, things will undoubtedly stay the same; she will continue to re-victimize herself over and over again.

Participants of IRIS are committed to change. The process is not easy and can be accomplished over time, and with the right guidance. Change is a step-by-step and day-by-day approach to living life without the baggage of the past.

## Solution Focused Therapy

I am a firm believer that I do not have the power to change people. No matter how much I try, no matter how motivating and inspirational I may be, and no matter how often I help people in their times of need, I do not have the power or authority to change anyone. In order for a person to change, she has to take the necessary steps to change the course of her life. I can offer a different perspective, but the individual receiving the information has to be ready to change.

Recognizing a person's readiness to change is a process and cannot be forced. When a person has been hurt, experienced trauma, or has been living in emotional pain for extended periods of time, she may develop an addiction to the pain. It's as if she expects people to fail her, hurt her, and even abandon her. Similar to the model created by Carlo DiClemente and J.O. Prochaska researchers in the field of addiction, IRIS participants may be in different stages of change, with each stage requiring a different level of treatment and intervention.

Helping a client find solutions to her existing problems requires the client to draw upon her individual strengths, skills, and abilities. Solution focused therapy is an outcome based approach to treatment first introduced by a team of family therapists led by Steve De Shazer and Insoo Kim Berg in the 1980's. In the course of their work, De Shazer and Berg realized that clients were more focused on arguing about the problems they were experiencing and pinning blame on others, or on their circumstances, rather than finding solutions to their problems. The shift in their clients' outcomes occurred when De Shazer and Berg changed their course of treatment by identifying areas in the client's life that seemed to bring about change, then developing solutions to effect those changes.

The same is true for IRIS. A participant does not focus on all that is wrong, or has gone wrong. She communicates a vision of what life would look like for her if things in her life changed. Incorporating solution focused therapy in the manifestation stage of transformation helps the participant develop an individual plan of action to initiate change.

In summary, each treatment approach used with the IRIS model is action-oriented. IRIS recognizes the need to take action in order to get desired results. The model is such a powerful model because the outcomes are measurable. The feedback that is received from IRIS participants has been a tremendous tool in transforming pain into possibility.

# ABOUT THE AUTHOR

Vashonna Etienne is a wife and mother of three wonderful children. She was born to a single mother in the Bronx and never had a relationship with her father.

Prior to pursuing her educational goals, Vashonna spent most of her adolescent years surviving in a community that wasn't always kid friendly. She grew up in a one bedroom apartment that housed five people including her mother, brother, and cousin, as well as her great aunt who is cognitively impaired. Her life circumstances were not favorable. She attributes her childhood as the motivating factor for pursuing her dreams of making an impact in the world.

Currently, Vashonna is the Founding Executive Director at The Center for Counseling and Holistic Services. She is a graduate of Hunter College, holds a Master's of Social Work, and is working toward her Doctorate in Social Work at Rutgers University. She is a practicing Licensed Clinical Social Worker in the State of New Jersey. Vashonna's experiences as a director of social services, and as a psychotherapist, have become the cornerstone of her professional and leadership development.

Vashonna is known to help women, men, and couples transform their pain into possibility. Her style is unique and refreshing as she helps people reach their greatest potential. With compassion and a commitment to the long term well-being of her clients, Vashonna adopts a wholesome clinical approach that is insightful, motivational, and inspirational.

www.ingramcontent.com/pod-product-compliance
Lightning Source LLC
Chambersburg PA
CBHW020017050426
42450CB00005B/514